EDGE
BOOKS

S0-AZR-431

LIFE ON THE
FRONT LINES

THE VIETNAM WAR ON THE FRONT LINES

by Tim Cooke

CAPSTONE PRESS
a capstone imprint

Edge Books are published by Capstone Press,
1710 Roe Crest Drive, North Mankato, Minnesota 56003
www.capstonepub.com

Published in 2014 by Capstone Publishers, Ltd.

Library of Congress Cataloging-in-Publication Data

Cooke, Tim, 1961-
The Vietnam War on the front lines / by Tim Cooke.
    pages cm. -- (Edge books. Life on the front lines)
Summary: "Approaches the topic of the Vietnam War from the perspective
of soldiers fighting in it"-- Provided by publisher.
ISBN 978-1-4914-0846-9 (library binding) -- ISBN 978-1-4914-0851-3
(pbk.)
1. Vietnam War, 1961-1975--Juvenile literature. 2. Vietnam War,
1961-1975--United States--Juvenile literature. I. Title.
DS557.7.C664 2015
959.704'340973--dc23

2013049461

For Brown Bear Books Ltd:
Editorial Director: Lindsey Lowe
Text: Tim Cooke
Children's Publisher: Anne O'Daly
Design Manager: Keith Davis
Designer: Lynne Lennon
Picture Manager: Sophie Mortimer
Production Director: Alastair Gourlay

Source Notes
p.9 Stephen W. Dant, interviewed by Richard Verrone, 2005, interview transcript (OH0418), Vietnam Archive: Lubbock, Texas, 13;
p.11 Haywood T. Kirkland, from www.historyisaweapon.com/defcon/kirkbloodsvietnam.html; **p.13** William C. Westmoreland, quoted
in Cath Senker, *The Vietnam War*, Capstone Global Library Ltd, 2012, p.32; **p.17** Gerald Kumpf, quoted in James Westheider, *Fighting
in Vietnam:The Experiences of the U.S. Soldier*, Stackpole Books, 2011, p.84; **p.19** John Ballweg, quoted in James Westheider, *Fighting in
Vietnam:The Experiences of the U.S. Soldier*, Stackpole Books, 2011, pp.84-85; **p.21** Jacqueline Navarro Rhoads, Jacqueline Rhoads, *Nurses
in Vietnam: The Forgotten Veterans*, Texas Monthly Press, 1987, p.13; **p.22** Gary F. Birkenmeier, quoted in Leo Daugherty, *Voices of Vietnam*,
The Brown Reference Group, 2003, p.148; **p.27** Willie L. Christian, quoted in James E. Westheider, *The Vietnam War*, Greenwood Press,
2007, p.91–92; **p.29** Priscilla Mosby, quoted in James E. Westheider, *The Vietnam War*, Greenwood Press, p.94.

Photo Credits
Front Cover: National Archives and Records Administration
Interior: All images National Archives and Records Administration except: **Everett Collection:** 27b; **Getty Images:** Keystone-France
24/25t, Larry Burrows/Time & Life Pictures 17tl, Rolls Press/Popperfoto 17br; **Library of Congress:** 8b; **Robert Hunt Library:** 5, 8/9, 9br.
Artistic Effects: Shutterstock

All Artworks © Brown Bear Books Ltd
Brown Bear Books has made every attempt to contact the copyright holder. If you have any
information please contact smortimer@windmillbooks.co.uk

Printed in China

TABLE OF CONTENTS

THE VIETNAM WAR

In the early 1960s the United States became involved in a civil war in Vietnam in Southeast Asia. After World War II (1939–1945), Vietnam was divided into two countries. North Vietnam was a **communist** state. South Vietnam was a French colony until 1954, when it became independent. When the North threatened to invade the South in the late 1950s, U.S. military advisers arrived to help train the South Vietnamese Army. U.S. politicians feared that communism might spread. They thought that would threaten U.S. influence in Asia.

A U.S. infantry patrol takes cover by a bush after coming under fire.

Vietcong guerrilla fighters celebrate the capture of a U.S. armored personnel carrier.

In 1965 the first U.S. ground troops arrived in Vietnam. The war escalated, and more U.S. troops arrived. U.S. aircraft launched a bombing campaign against North Vietnam. Meanwhile the North Vietnamese trained and supplied the Vietcong. These **guerrilla** fighters lived secretly in the South and launched attacks on enemy targets.

The Vietnam War was unpopular in the United States. In 1968 Richard Nixon was elected president on his promise to withdraw U.S. troops. In June 1973 U.S. involvement in the war ended. Nearly two years later, North Vietnamese tanks rolled into the Southern capital, Saigon. Vietnam was reunited as a communist country.

- **communist:** following a political system in which all property is owned by the state and allocated to individuals

- **guerrilla:** a soldier who fights by means of tactics such as ambush, sabotage, or murder

CHAPTER 1

THE MAKING OF A SOLDIER

When the United States first sent advisers to Vietnam in the late 1950s, it intended to limit its role in the conflict. The U.S. government did not want to fight a war, but conflict soon escalated. By 1967 almost 500,000 U.S. troops were in Vietnam. Although most soldiers were volunteers, such a huge army could only be sustained by forcing people into service. More than 2.2 million soldiers were called up through the **draft**.

Helicopters drop U.S. soldiers to begin a patrol in Vietnam. Recruits were trained for a new style of war. They needed to be highly mobile.

The first U.S. Marines to arrive in Vietnam in March 1965 set up camp on a sports field. Soon U.S. forces constructed huge bases that were well defended from attacks by the enemy.

These soldiers were from communities across the United States. Many of them had never been outside the country before. All the soldiers had to be trained to be able to face an elusive enemy. Soldiers had to be fit enough to serve in the hot conditions of Southeast Asia. The new recruits also had to become used to the discipline of being in the military.

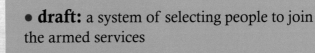

● **draft:** a system of selecting people to join the armed services

RECRUITMENT AND THE DRAFT

At the start of U.S. involvement in Vietnam, most Americans supported the draft. The majority of military personnel in Vietnam were volunteers. But as **call-ups** grew, the draft became seen as unfair. Many draftees were African-Americans from poor families. They suffered two-thirds of all combat deaths. Many Americans did not want to go to war. Anti-draft protests became common. In 1971 more than 300,000 people marched in Washington, D.C., against the draft.

U.S. government officials draw balls to decide which men are drafted. Many people saw the draft as unfair. Rich or well-educated men were often able to avoid service.

Americans protest against the war. Men who received draft cards ordering them to report for service burned them in public. This action was against the law.

Police carry away an antiwar protestor. As opposition to the Vietnam War grew, the country split into those who supported the war and those who opposed it.

EYEWITNESS

NAME: Stephen W. Dant
UNIT: 5th Battalion, 198th Brigade

" They said 'We're drafting into the Marines this morning. One of you six guys is going to be a Marine, any volunteers?' They took the fourth guy alphabetically. "

- **call-up:** an order to report for military service

TRAINING

New recruits began service with eight weeks of basic training at a boot camp. Boot camps were tough. Soldiers learned all kinds of things, from how to shine their boots to how to fire their M-14 rifles and how to use a map and compass. Most of all, soldiers had to learn to obey orders. There was further training for specialties such as **artillery** training or engineering. In Vietnam the recruits had two weeks of training in how to recognize the tactics of the Vietcong guerrillas.

Infantry recruits train with rifles at a camp in the United States.

• **artillery:** large weapons such as cannons and mortars

10

This platform in Vietnam was used to train soldiers for parachute landings.

Recruits in the United States received specialist training in recognizing and handling different types of explosive shells and grenades.

MUNITIONS IDENTIFICATION AND CHARACTERISTICS

SP6 MASSEY

TRANSPORTATION

The Vietnam War was the first war to be dominated by the helicopter. Helicopters were the best way to get to remote mountain and jungle bases. The most common type of helicopter was the "Huey," the nickname of the Bell UH-1 Iroquois. Hueys flew troops into and out of hostile territory. They evacuated more than 500,000 injured soldiers, and delivered supplies and mail. Other helicopters included heavily armed gunships used to attack enemy positions. More than 12,000 helicopters were used in Vietnam.

The Chinook was a transport helicopter that carried large numbers of troops or even tanks or artillery pieces.

" The most spectacular development was the coming of age of the helicopters. It saved innumerable lives through air evacuation. It gave us a battlefield mobility that we never dreamed of years previously. "

A patrol has its guns ready as a Huey prepares to take off. This was when a helicopter was most vulnerable to attack.

U.S. soldiers board a passenger airliner for their flight home from Vietnam.

CHAPTER 2

AT THE FRONT

The war in Vietnam was not like any other war U.S. forces had fought. There was no front line in Vietnam. The communists' guerrilla tactics meant that the enemy could be anywhere. Enemy fighters were hard to tell apart from civilians. There were very few conventional battles, in which two sides faced one another in combat.

The U.S. Army adapted its **strategy** to the new type of warfare. First, it set up temporary fire bases around the country. These were well-protected bases in strategically important but isolated rural areas.

U.S. Marines shelter in a trench during an enemy artillery bombardment.

● **strategy:** a careful plan to achieve overall military victory, usually over a long period rather than in a single battle

Second, the infantry were sent out on patrols to try to find the enemy. Foot patrols became the most hated part of the war because of enemy ambushes and booby traps.

Not every soldier sent to Vietnam saw action. Only about one-fifth (80,000) of the army came up against the enemy. Most soldiers served in a support role. The standard length of service was one year. Soldiers counted down the days until they could return home.

In areas that were relatively safe from the enemy, U.S. troops lived in tents set up in large bases. The bases were surrounded by barriers for protection from enemy attacks.

FOOD AND DRINK

On large bases soldiers ate favorites from home such as hamburgers and fries. On patrol, life was very different. Soldiers carried C-rations in their packs. These precooked meals could be eaten hot or cold. Each C ration contained a meat item, vegetables and fruit, bread or crackers, and a dessert. A soldier was allowed three per day. Drinking water tasted horrible because it had purification tablets added to it. More popular drinks were beer or Coca-Cola. Coffee was drunk black because milk soured quickly in the heat.

U.S. soldiers enjoy fresh pineapple. Many soldiers bought fresh food from local people.

Soldiers at a forward position examine their C-rations. The rations were not popular, but each provided valuable energy and nutrition for the men.

Soldiers wait in line for food. This was a rare chance for forward troops to enjoy a nutritious meal instead of C-rations.

LIVING CONDITIONS

How a soldier lived depended on his rank, unless he was at a forward base, such as a fire base. On permanent bases, officers had private or semi-private rooms in huts. Lower ranks shared tents that were erected on cement or wooden floors. Larger permanent camps had washing facilities, a snack bar, post office, grocery store, barbershop, swimming pool, recreation center, library, and even a souvenir store. However, on patrol or in remote fire bases, all ranks often had to sleep together in foxholes hollowed out of the ground.

A soldier washes at a forward base. Water was left out in the sun during the day to heat up.

Fire bases were heavily fortified. They had few recreation facilities and few comforts for soldiers.

A soldier cools off during a patrol. All drinking water had to be purified before it was used to make sure it was free from disease-causing bacteria.

EYEWITNESS

NAME: John R. Ballweg
RANK: Warrant Officer, 11th Armored Cavalry Regiment

" We had fairly decent food... nothing to write home about. [The meals] weren't like going to Outback or something like that. They were passable. "

MEDICINE AND HEALTH

During World War II, one in three wounded soldiers died. In Vietnam, that rate fell to one in five. The improvement was due largely to the helicopter. It was used to get injured soldiers to the nearest field hospital, often within 20 minutes. In 1965 there were just two military hospitals in Vietnam, each with 100 beds. By 1969 this had increased to 30 hospitals with 5,000 beds. Soldiers did not only face injuries from enemy action. There were leeches, scorpions, and poisonous snakes. Poor **hygiene** also caused disease.

> A nurse prepares a vaccination. More than 5,000 nurses volunteered to serve in Vietnam.

• **hygiene:** the degree to which people keep themselves or their surrounding clean, especially to prevent disease

Australian troops receive vaccinations in Vietnam. The Australians fought on the same side as the U.S. troops.

A combat medical team rushes a casualty to a waiting Huey to be evacuated to a field hospital for further treatment.

UNDER FIRE

Vietcong and North Vietnamese tactics were to launch ambushes or bomb attacks. U.S. forces tried to locate the enemy before they struck. Commanders adopted a tactic called search and destroy. Foot patrols set out to locate the enemy and their bases. These patrols were very tense. Soldiers dreaded the booby traps the Vietcong placed along the routes. They included pits full of sharpened stakes. The Vietcong also launched ambushes from the jungles. Helicopters flew soldiers into enemy territory, but could not remove the need to patrol through the countryside on foot.

Men from the U.S. 1st Infantry Division come under sniper fire on a patrol in 1965.

A U.S. Marine machine-gun team opens fire. One soldier of the two-man team fired the gun. The other soldier loaded ammunition.

A U.S. patrol and some terrified South Vietnamese children take cover from enemy fire in a ditch.

CHAPTER 3

SPIRIT AND MORALE

The Vietnam War was unpopular, both with the soldiers who fought it and U.S. civilians. As a result, **morale** among soldiers was often low. In addition, it eventually became clear that the war was probably unwinnable. The United States was fighting a war the French had already given up on. For soldiers, low morale made their year-long tour of duty even more difficult.

A U.S. Marine relaxes with a comic book. Reading was a popular way for soldiers to pass the time.

Soldiers in Vietnam receive letters from home. The arrival of the mail was a highlight of any day, and the U.S. Army made sure it reached the soldiers as often as possible.

Many soldiers had been drafted against their will. They were far from home, fighting in a country they knew nothing about, for a cause they did not understand. Their mood switched between boredom and terror. They suffered great psychological stress.

Soldiers tried to keep their spirits up. Writing or receiving letters helped them cope with homesickness. Soldiers often made strong friendships with their comrades.

As the war went on, soldiers became more disillusioned. They heard about the opposition to the war at home. Falling morale led to a lack of discipline. Fragging became more common, although it was still quite rare. This was the deliberate killing or wounding of an officer in order to avoid obeying his orders.

● **morale:** the fighting spirit of a person or group, and how confident they feel of winning a victory

KEEPING IN TOUCH

Many U.S. soldiers wrote home and received mail on a regular basis. In remote camps mail was delivered by helicopter. Soldiers were supposed to destroy the letters they received in case the enemy captured them. But many soldiers disobeyed these orders. They kept their letters to re-read. Technology also allowed soldiers to make satellite phone calls using the Military Auxiliary Radio System (MARS). Long lines formed for the chance to make a call home.

Soldiers write home outside their "hooch," or shelter. They have employed local women to clean for them.

Packages arrive in Vietnam. Many families mailed cassette tapes to soldiers so they could hear the voices of their loved ones.

RECREATION

The United Service Organizations (USO) was set up during World War II. It entertained troops in Vietnam too. At its peak, 17 USO clubs entertained 1 million service personnel each month. The USO brought movie and entertainment stars such as Bob Hope, Ann-Margret, Raquel Welch, and John Wayne to Vietnam to entertain the troops. Beginning in 1966, star players from the National Football League (NFL) also came. Soldiers relaxed at USO clubs during their leave. Each club had a store, a barber, and hot showers. Soldiers spent their time reading, playing pool, writing letters, or just hanging out.

Hollywood star Bob Hope introduces the current Miss U.S.A. at a USO Christmas show at An Khe.

A U.S. soldier relaxes next to his machine gun. Men seized any chance they had to relax for a moment.

EYEWITNESS

NAME: Priscilla Mosby
OCCUPATION: Band singer
PLACE: Vietnam bases

"Without electricity, we had to just rough it, and that was even more fun ... If you played bass, you would stand up there and go 'Da-Dom-Dom-Dom' and make the sound with your mouth. It was beautiful."

A huge audience watches entertainer Sammy Davis Jr. on a tour of U.S. bases in Vietnam.

GLOSSARY

artillery (arr-till-er-EE)—large, heavy guns, such as cannons and mortars

call-up (CAWL-up)—an order to report for military service

communist (KAHM-yuh-nist)—following a political system in which there is no private property

draft (DRAFT)—a system of selecting people to join the armed services

guerrilla (ger-ILL-uh)—a soldier who fights by means of tactics such as ambush, sabotage, or murder

hygiene (HYE-jeen)—the degree to which people keep themselves or their surrounding clean, especially to avoid disease

infantry (IN-fuhn-tree)—soldiers who usually fight on foot

morale (muh-RAL)—the fighting spirit of a person or group, and how confident they feel of winning a victory

strategy (STRAT-uh-jee)—a careful plan to achieve overall military victory, usually over a long period rather than in a single battle

READ MORE

Cooke, Tim. *The Experience of War. Nam: The Vietnam War.* Tucson, AZ: Brown Bear Books, 2013.

Gitlin, Martin. *U.S. Involvement in Vietnam*. Essential Events. Edina, MN: Abdo Publishing, 2010.

Kent, Deborah. *The Vietnam War from Da Nang to Saigon.* The United States at War. Berkeley Heights, NJ: Enslow Publishing Inc., 2011.

Perritano, John. *Vietnam War.* America at War. New York: Franklin Watts, 2010.

Samuels, Charlie. *Timeline of the Vietnam War*. Americans at War. New York: Gareth Stevens Publishing, 2012.

Tougas, Shelley. *Weapons, Gear, and Uniforms of the Vietnam War*. Equipped for Battle. Mankato, MN: Capstone Press, 2012.

INTERNET SITES

FactHound offers a safe, fun way to find Internet sites related to this book. All of the sites on FactHound have been researched by our staff.

Here's all you do:

Visit *www.facthound.com*a

Type in this code: 9781491408469

Super-cool stuff! Check out projects, games and lots more at **www.capstonekids.com**

INDEX